How to Draw
FOREST ANIMALS

Barbara Soloff Levy

DOVER PUBLICATIONS, INC.
Mineola, New York

Bibliographical Note

How to Draw Forest Animals is a new work, first published by
Dover Publications, Inc., in 2007.

International Standard Book Number

ISBN-13: 978-0-486-47199-0
ISBN-10: 0-486-47199-3

Manufactured in the United States by RR Donnelley
47199308   2016
www.doverpublications.com

Note

The forest is full of creatures—and you can find pictures of thirty of them in this fun-to-use and instructive book. There are large animals—the black bear and the moose—and small ones, such as the skunk and the raccoon. A few are tiny and hard to spot, like the chipmunk and the white-footed mouse. And watch out for the corn snake, which slithers through the leaves! Wherever you wander in the forest, you will see many interesting sights hidden among the trees, rocks, and streams.

Each drawing is made of shapes and lines. Begin with the part of the animal at the top of the page, and then add on more shapes and lines as shown. You will be erasing the dotted lines in some pictures, so use a pencil, not a pen. You may want to trace the steps of each picture first, just to get a feel for drawing. Be sure to use the helpful Practice Pages, opposite the drawing pages.

When you have finished all of the drawings in the book, you can go over the lines with a felt-tip pen or colored pencil. Erase the dotted lines when you get to the last step in the drawings. Finally, you can color in your drawings any way you wish. Why not try to make up some drawings of your own when you're done? Have fun!

2   Skunk

Practice Page

4   Opossum

6   Black Bear

Practice Page

Practice Page

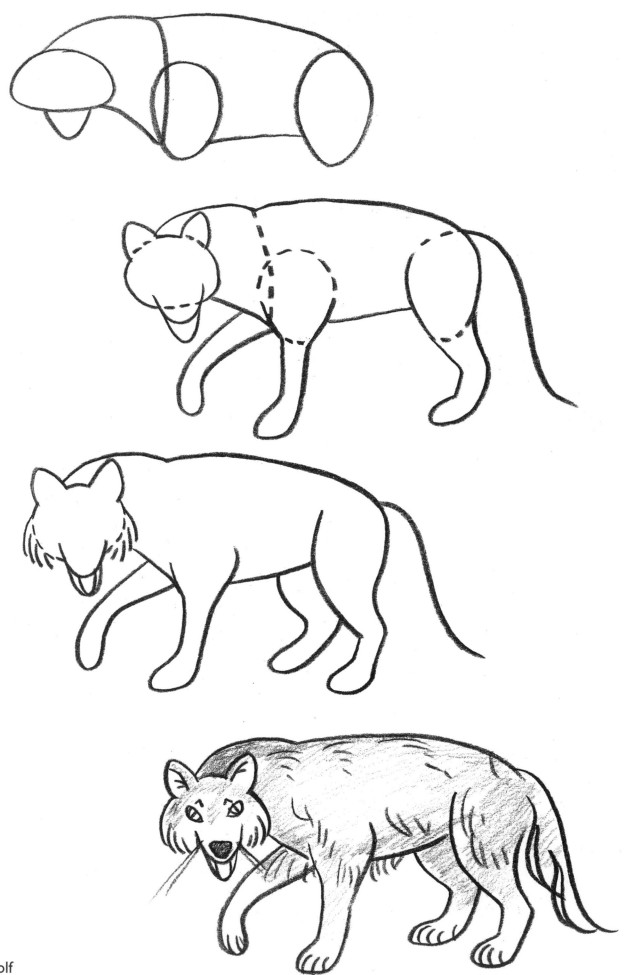

8　Wolf

Practice Page

10   Red Fox

Practice Page

12 Porcupine

Practice Page

14   Beaver

Practice Page

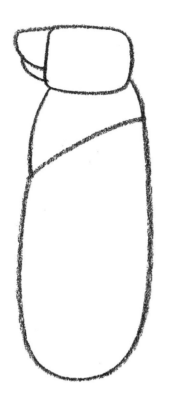
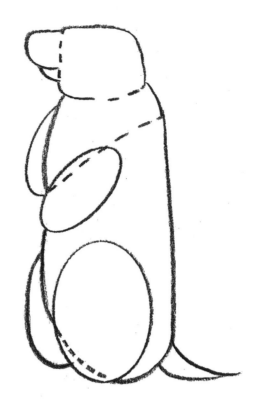

18   Woodchuck

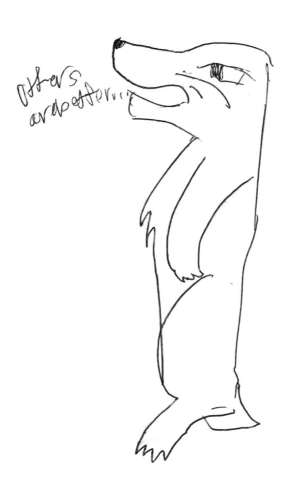

Otters
are better...

22   Deer

24   Moose

Practice Page

26   Squirrel

28   Chipmunk

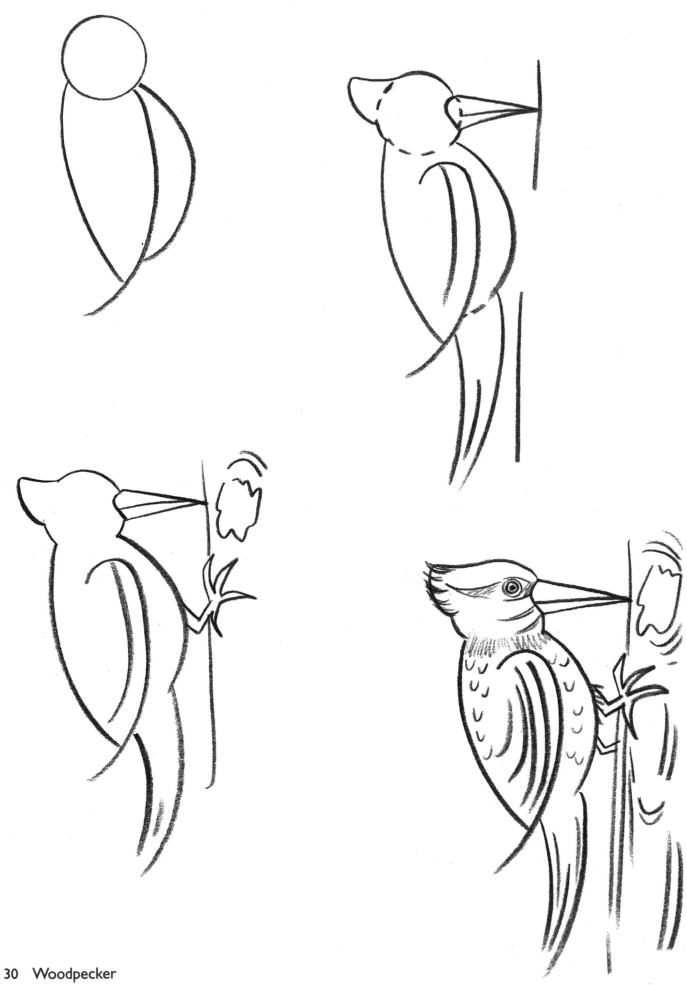

30 Woodpecker

Practice Page

Practice Page

Practice Page

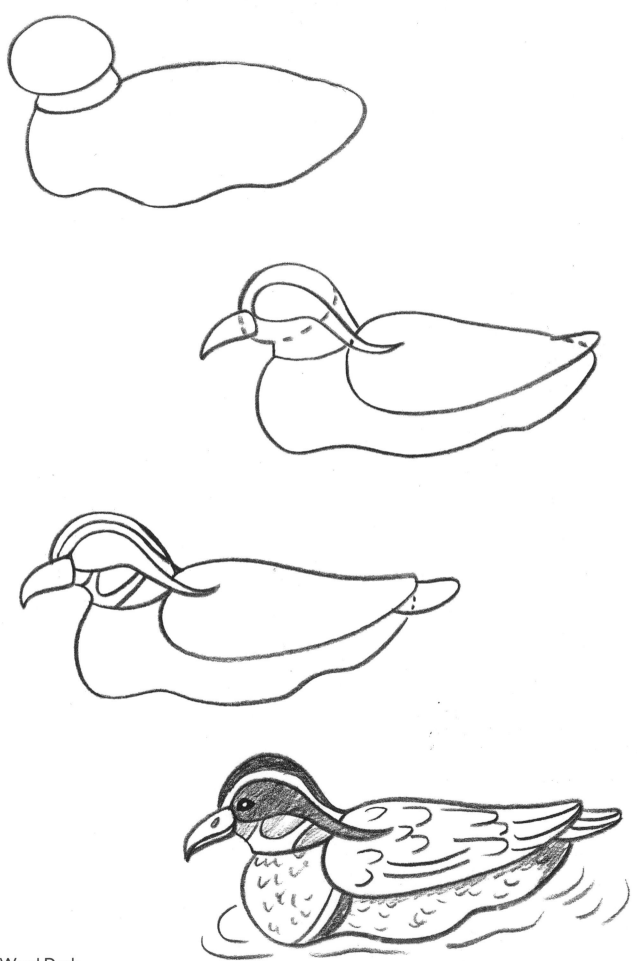

34   Wood Duck

Practice Page

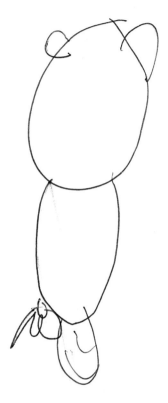

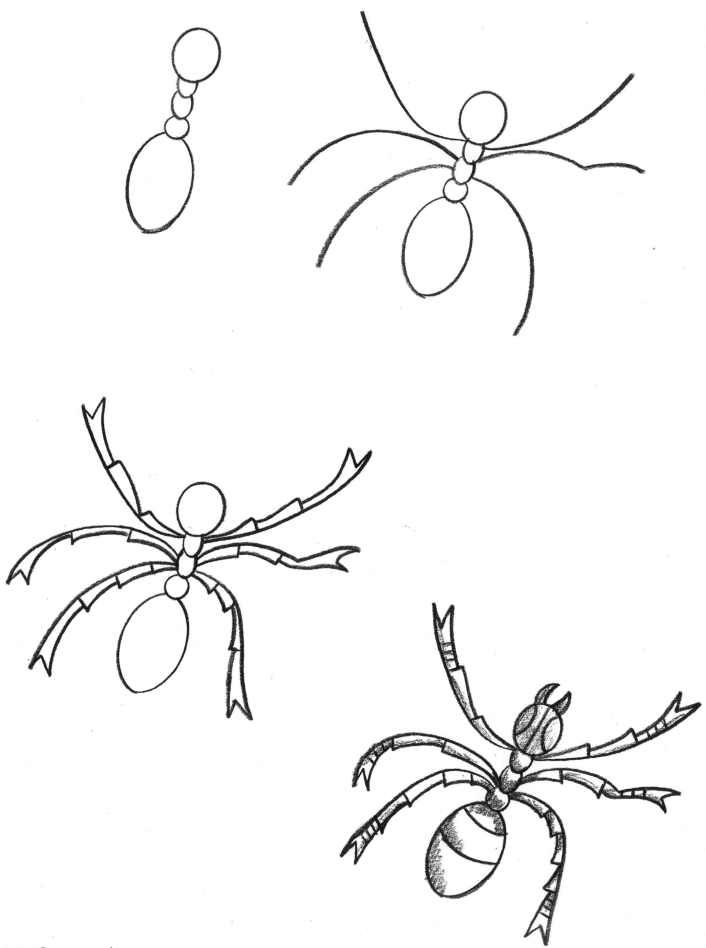

Practice Page

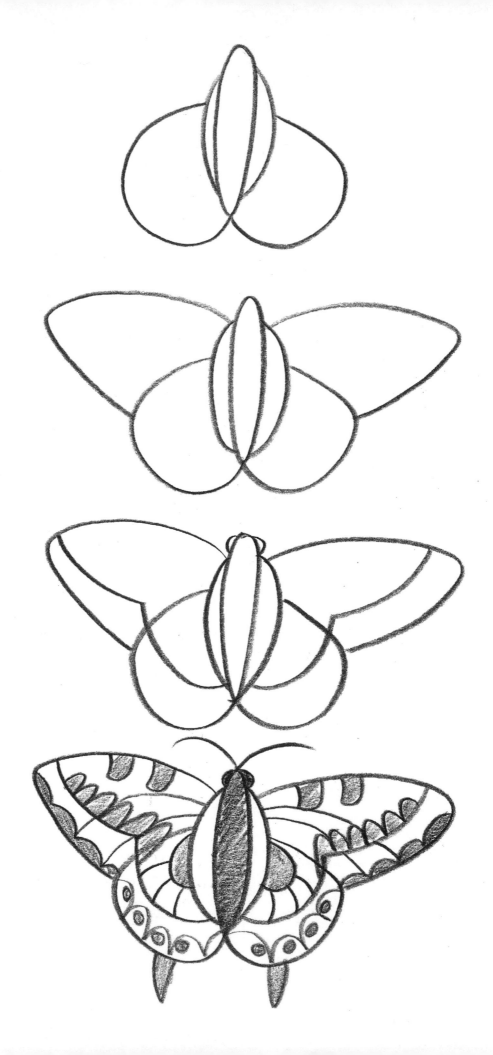

50   White-footed Mouse

Practice Page

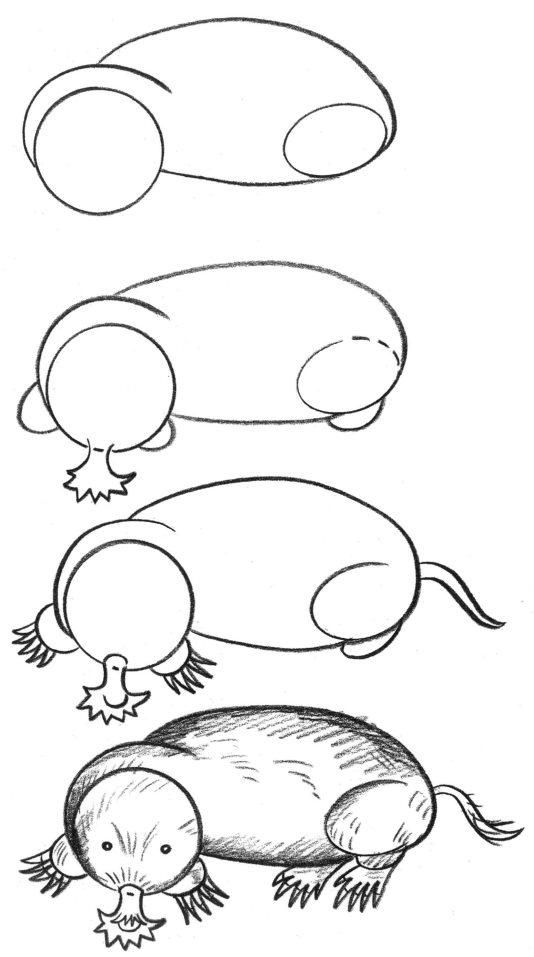

Practice Page

Practice Page

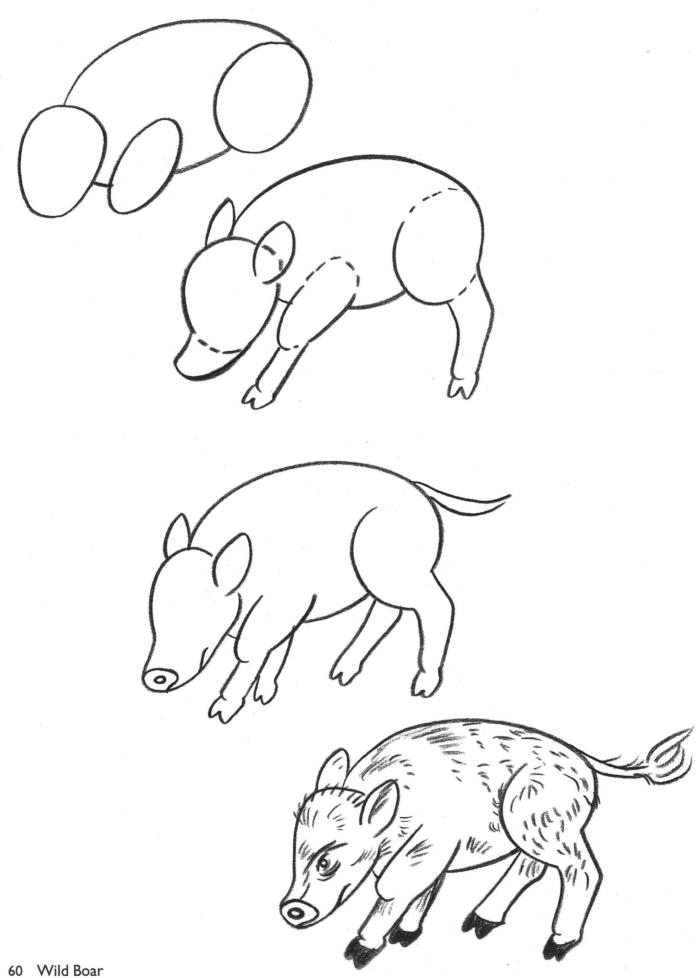

60　Wild Boar

Practice Page

Practice Page